Leadership and the One Minute Manager

Also by the Authors

Also by Ken Blanchard
TRUST WORKS! (with Cynthia Olmstead
and Martha Lawrence), 2013
LEAD YOUR FAMILY LIKE JESUS (with Tricia Goyer
and Phil Hodges), 2013
GREAT LEADERS GROW (with Mark Miller), 2012
MANAGEMENT OF ORGANIZATIONAL BEHAVIOR
(with Paul Hersey), 10th edition, 2012
LEAD WITH LUV (with Colleen Barrett), 2011
WHO KILLED CHANGE? (with John Britt, Judd Hoekstra,
and Pat Zigarmi), 2009
HELPING PEOPLE WIN AT WORK (with Garry Ridge), 2009
WHALE DONE PARENTING (with Chuck Tompkins, Thad
Lacinak, and Jim Ballard), 2009
THE ONE MINUTE ENTREPRENEUR (with Don Hutson and
Ethan Willis), 2008
THE 4TH SECRET OF THE ONE MINUTE MANAGER (with
Margret McBride), 2008
THE MOST LOVING PLACE IN TOWN (with Phil Hodges), 2008
LEAD LIKE JESUS (with Phil Hodges), 2007
LEADING AT A HIGHER LEVEL (with the Founding Associates
and Consulting Partners of The Ken Blanchard Companies), 2007
KNOW CAN DO (with Paul Meyer and Dick Ruhe), 2007
THE MULLIGAN (with Wally Armstrong), 2007
THE ON-TIME, ON-TARGET MANAGER
(with Steve Gottry), 2004
SELF LEADERSHIP AND THE ONE MINUTE MANAGER
(with Susan Fowler and Laurence Hawkins), 2005
ONE SOLITARY LIFE, 2005
GO TEAM! (with Alan Randolph and Peter Glazier), 2005
THE SECRET (with Mark Miller), 2004
CUSTOMER MANIA! (with Fred Finch and Jim Ballard), 2004
THE LEADERSHIP PILL (with Mark Muchnick), 2003
FULL STEAM AHEAD! (with Jesse Stoner), 2003
THE SERVANT LEADER (with Phil Hodges), 2003

ZAP THE GAPS! (with Dana Robinson and Jim Robinson), 2002

WHALE DONE! (with Thad Lacinak, Chuck Tompkins,
and Jim Ballard), 2002

THE GENEROSITY FACTOR (with Truett Cathy), 2002

HIGH FIVE! (with Sheldon Bowles, Donald Carew,
and Eunice Parisi-Carew), 2001

BIG BUCKS! (with Sheldon Bowles), 2000

THE ONE MINUTE MANAGER BALANCES WORK AND LIFE
(with Dee Edington and Marjorie Blanchard), 1999

THE ONE MINUTE GOLFER, 1999

LEADERSHIP BY THE BOOK (with Bill Hybels
and Phil Hodges), 1999

THE 3 KEYS TO EMPOWERMENT (with John Carlos
and Alan Randolph), 1999

LEADERSHIP BY THE BOOK (with Bill Hybels
and Phil Hodges), 1999

THE HEART OF A LEADER, 1999

MANAGING BY VALUES (with Michael O'Connor), 1998

GUNG HO! (with Sheldon Bowles), 1998

MISSION POSSIBLE (with Terry Waghorn), 1996

EMPOWERMENT TAKES MORE THAN A MINUTE
(with John Carlos and Alan Randolph), 1996

EVERYONE'S A COACH (with Don Shula), 1995

RAVING FANS (with Sheldon Bowles), 1993

THE ONE MINUTE MANAGER BUILDS HIGH PERFORMING
TEAMS (with Don Carew and Eunice Parisi-Carew), 1990

THE ONE MINUTE MANAGER MEETS THE MONKEY
(with William Oncken Jr., and Hal Burrows), 1989

THE POWER OF ETHICAL MANAGEMENT
(with Norman Vincent Peale), 1988

PUTTING THE ONE MINUTE MANAGER TO WORK (with
Robert Lorber), 1984

THE ONE MINUTE MANAGER (with Spencer Johnson), 1982

Also by Drea Zigarmi
THE LEADER WITHIN (with Ken Blanchard, Michael O'Connor, Carl Edeburn), 2007
THE TEAM LEADER'S IDEA-A-DAY GUIDE (with Susan Fowler), 1997

Also by Patricia Zigarmi
WHO KILLED CHANGE? (with Ken Blanchard, John Britt, Judd Hoekstra), 2009

Leadership and the One Minute Manager

Increasing Effectiveness Through
Situational Leadership® II

UPDATED EDITION

Ken Blanchard
Patricia Zigarmi
Drea Zigarmi

WILLIAM MORROW
An Imprint of HarperCollins*Publishers*

The Ken Blanchard Companies retains the exclusive rights to any training applications of the SLII® model.

HarperCollins books may be purchased for educational, business, or sales promotional use. For information, please e-mail the Special Markets Department at SPsales@harpercollins.com.

FIRST EDITION

Library of Congress Cataloging-in-Publication data has been applied for.

ISBN 978-0-06-230944-0

17   OV/RRD   10

The Symbol

The One Minute Manager's symbol—a one-minute readout from the face of a digital watch— is intended to remind each of us to take a minute out of our day to look into the faces of the people we lead. And to realize that *they* are our most importance resource.

Introduction

PAUL Hersey and I began developing Situational Leadership® at Ohio University in the late 1960s and then wrote about it extensively in our textbook, *Management of Organizational Behavior: Utilizing Human Resources*, now in its tenth edition from Prentice-Hall. In the early 1980s my coauthors, Pat and Drea Zigarmi, and I, together with the other founding associates of The Ken Blanchard Companies, made a number of changes in the model. The changes reflected our own experience, the ideas managers shared with us, and the findings of research we'd been conducting. The result was a new generation of Situational Leadership® thinking, which we call Situational Leadership® II.

Situational Leadership® II's practical, easy-to-understand and apply approach to leading and developing people has been taught over the last thirty years to leaders at all levels of most Fortune 1000 companies, as well as to leaders in fast-growing entrepreneurial organizations throughout the world.

This new, updated edition of *Leadership and the One Minute Manager* reflects our latest thinking about Situational Leadership® II. Written as a parable, it tells the story of an overworked entrepreneur who learns from the One Minute Manager how to get the most out of a diverse team by becoming a situational leader.

Pat, Drea, and I hope this will be a book you will read and reread until being a situational leader becomes second nature to you in your leadership roles at work, in your home, and in the community.

—KEN BLANCHARD, coauthor of *The One Minute Manager® and Leading at a Higher Level*

In memory of

our friend and colleague

Paul Hersey

for

his genius and creativity

in the development of the original

Situational Leadership®

Contents

THE One Minute Manager got a call one day from a woman who said she was an entrepreneur. He was glad to hear from her, because he always enjoyed talking to people who had the courage to start their own businesses.

The entrepreneur explained that she was having a hard time finding people who were willing to work as hard as she was.

"I feel I have to do everything myself. I can't count on anyone to take on some of the things that need to be done," said the entrepreneur.

"What you have to do," said the One Minute Manager, "is learn to delegate."

"But my people are not ready," said the entrepreneur.

"Then you need to train them," said the One Minute Manager.

"But I don't have time," said the entrepreneur.

"If that's the case," said the One Minute Manager with a grin, "you do have a problem. Why don't you come over this afternoon and we'll have a talk."

WHEN the entrepreneur arrived at the One Minute Manager's office that afternoon, she found him talking to his assistant at her desk.

"I appreciate your willingness to meet with me," said the entrepreneur as she joined the One Minute Manager in his office.

"It's my pleasure," said the One Minute Manager. "I've heard that you have been very successful in a number of ventures. What do you think it takes to be successful?"

"It's really quite easy," the entrepreneur said with a smile. "All you have to do is work half a day. You can work either the first twelve hours or the second twelve hours."

After he'd had a good laugh, the One Minute Manager said, "While I think the amount of time and effort you put into work is important, I'm afraid too many people think there is a direct relationship between the amount of work they do and success—the more time they put in, the more successful they will be."

"I thought you would say that," said the entrepreneur. "In fact, I understand one of your favorite quotes is:

*

*Don't
Work
Harder—
Work
Smarter*

*

"Absolutely," said the One Minute Manager. "But before talking about my thoughts on working smarter, let me ask you one more question."

"Ask away," said the entrepreneur.

"You call yourself an entrepreneur," said the One Minute Manager. "What does that mean to you?"

The entrepreneur smiled and said, "A friend of mine described beautifully what it means to be an entrepreneur. He told me he once took his senior vice president to the top of a hill that overlooked the city. It was a beautiful view.

"He said to his vice president, 'Do you see that ridge down there? Wouldn't that be a great place to build a house?'

"'It sure would be,' said his vice president.

"'Can you imagine a pool over to the right? Wouldn't that be something?' continued my friend.

"'Just tremendous,' said the vice president.

"'How about a tennis court to the left?' said my friend.

"'What a setting,' said the vice president.

"'Let me tell you one thing,' said my friend. 'If you continue to work as hard as you have and accomplish all the goals we have set, I guarantee that someday—someday, all of that will be mine.'"

"That's funny," said the One Minute Manager with a big smile on his face. "But I think that story illustrates some of your problems with managing and motivating others."

"What do you mean?" asked the entrepreneur.

"LET me explain it this way," said the One Minute Manager. "I would imagine your organization looks like a pyramid with you, as the CEO, at the top and all your individual contributors at the bottom. In between are several levels of management."

"That's the way it's organized," said the entrepreneur. "Is there something wrong with a pyramidal organization?"

"No," said the One Minute Manager. "There is nothing wrong with it as an organizational chart. The trouble comes when you think and operate with a traditional top-down philosophy."

"I don't think I follow you," said the entrepreneur.

"When you think with a top-down pyramid philosophy," said the One Minute Manager, "the assumption is that everyone works for the person above them on the organizational ladder. As a result, managers are thought to be 'responsible' for planning, organizing, and evaluating everything that happens in the organization, while their people are supposed to be 'responsive to the directives of management.' That's why people like you end up thinking managers do all the work."

"How should it be?" asked the entrepreneur.

"I prefer to turn the pyramid upside down, so that top managers are at the bottom," said the One Minute Manager. "When that happens, there is a subtle but powerful twist in who is responsible and who should be responsive to whom."

"In other words, you're saying managers should work for their people, and not the reverse."

"Precisely," said the One Minute Manager. "When it comes to implementation, if you think your people are responsible and that your job is to be responsive to them, you really work hard to provide them with the resources they need to accomplish the goals you've agreed to. You realize your job is not to do all the work yourself or to sit back and wait to 'catch them doing something wrong,' but to roll up your sleeves and help them accomplish their goals. If you do that, both of you are successful."

"But as I told you earlier," said the entrepreneur, "I don't have time to be responsive to the needs of all my people."

"You don't have to work closely with all your people," said the One Minute Manager, "only those who need your direction and support to develop their competence and commitment."

"You mean you treat people differently?" wondered the entrepreneur.

"Absolutely," said the One Minute Manager. "There's a saying we use around here that says it all:

*

*Different Strokes
For
Different Folks*

*

"IF that's true," asked the entrepreneur, "how do you treat your people differently?"

"Why don't you talk to some of them?" suggested the One Minute Manager. "They can tell you about my leadership styles."

"Leadership styles with an S?" asked the entrepreneur.

"Your leadership style is the way you work with someone," said the One Minute Manager. "It's how you behave, over time, when you're trying to influence the performance of others, as perceived by them. You'll see that my team members see me using more than one leadership style."

"Is your leadership style the way you think you behave," asked the entrepreneur, "or the way others say you behave?"

"Let me explain it this way," said the One Minute Manager. "If you think you are an empathetic, people-oriented manager, but your people think you are a hard-nosed, task-oriented person, whose perception of reality will they use— yours or their own?"

"Obviously their own," said the entrepreneur.

"Right," said the One Minute Manager. "Your perception of how you lead is interesting, but it tells you only how you intend to act. Unless it matches the perceptions of others, it is not very helpful. That's why I want you to talk to some of my people. They'll give you a good read on my leadership style—or should I say styles—so you can see if I really treat people differently."

With that, he turned to his computer, printed out a list of six names, and handed it to the entrepreneur.

"Here's a list of the people in this building who are on my team," said the One Minute Manager. "Pick any name. Talk to any of them."

"Let me start with Larry McKenzie," said the entrepreneur as she looked at the list. "Perhaps he can connect me with the others I want to talk to."

"I'm sure he can," said the One Minute Manager, smiling. "You may have to catch them in an airport between flights or schedule an early morning call, but I'm sure they'll find the time to talk."

"Since Larry's in the building, maybe I can ask your assistant to call and find out if he's available," said the entrepreneur.

"Great idea," said the One Minute Manager. "Then she can tell you where his office is."

The entrepreneur smiled. "How about I check back in with you later this afternoon?"

"Sure," said the One Minute Manager. "Just confirm the meeting with my assistant. I'll look forward to hearing about what you discover."

THE entrepreneur was feeling good as she headed toward Larry McKenzie's office. She was glad she had decided to come to see the One Minute Manager. His assistant had been very helpful and was able to squeeze her into Larry's schedule when one of his morning meetings was canceled. *I have a feeling I will learn some useful things here,* she thought to herself.

When she got to Larry's office, she found a man in his late thirties. He was the vice president for people and talent development for the company.

After they exchanged greetings, Larry smiled. "I understand you've been visiting with the One Minute Manager. What can I do for you?"

"I'm interested in finding out how the One Minute Manager works with you," said the entrepreneur. "Would you call him a collaborative manager? I've been reading a lot about collaborative leadership."

"He's far from being collaborative with me," said Larry. "In fact, he is very directive with me. People development is his baby. So my job is essentially to follow his direction."

"But why doesn't he just assign you the projects he needs you to do and then just let you figure them out?" wondered the entrepreneur. "He must trust you if he put you in this job."

"I think he trusts that I'll develop in this role, but he's the expert," said Larry. "So he assigns me projects and then works very closely with me on almost every aspect of them. This role is a big stretch for me. I'm just learning about several of the responsibilities that come with this job."

"Don't you resent that?" asked the entrepreneur. "It sounds pretty controlling to me."

"Not at all," said Larry. "I was in comp and benefits before I got this position three months ago. I jumped at the opportunity to move into the people and talent group. Working with the One Minute Manager would give me a chance to learn the whole area of talent development from the ground up. He's considered a real pro when it comes to developing people. So apart from comp and benefits—where he leaves me alone when he works with me—in almost every other area, he's very clear about what he wants me to do and how he wants me to do it. I always know where I stand, because of the frequent meetings we have and the ongoing feedback he gives me."

"Do you think he will ever let you make any decisions on your own?" asked the entrepreneur.

"As I learn the ropes," said Larry. "But it's hard to make good decisions when I don't know a lot about what it takes to accomplish my goals. Right now I'm glad the One Minute Manager wants to be involved. I'm excited about my job, and as I gain experience, I'm sure I'll assume more responsibility."

"Does the One Minute Manager manage everyone who reports to him the way he manages you?" asked the entrepreneur.

"No," said Larry. "Why don't you talk with Cindy Liu, our director of finance? The One Minute Manager works with her very differently. I'll text her and see if she can meet with you."

Cindy texted Larry back almost immediately to say that she had fifteen minutes right now between flights and if Larry and the entrepreneur went to her office, her assistant would reach her on her mobile.

When the entrepreneur and Larry got to Cindy's office, Cindy's assistant invited them to sit as she got Cindy on the phone. After Larry introduced the two women and left, the entrepreneur began. "Larry says that the One Minute Manager leads you differently than he does him. Is that true?"

"Absolutely," said Cindy. "We operate as colleagues on almost everything related to the financial management of the company. The One Minute Manager never tells me what to do, but together we decide on the direction we want to take."

"Sounds like he is very collaborative with you," said the entrepreneur.

"Very much so," said Cindy. "I get a lot of support and encouragement from the One Minute Manager. What I find him doing is listening to me and drawing me out. He asks great questions and helps me think about options. He also shares lots of information about his vision and about his knowledge of the company with me. It's a perfect working relationship for me. I've been working in finance for over fifteen years, so it feels good to be treated as a competent, contributing member of a team. I've worked for some other people who certainly didn't make me feel like that."

"From talking to you," said the entrepreneur, "I'm beginning to believe that the One Minute Manager is either controlling or collaborative. With Larry he is very directive and hands-on, and with you, he treats you like an equal and is very supportive."

"Don't draw any conclusions about those being his only two styles," said Cindy, "until you talk to John DaLapa, our director of operations."

"You mean the One Minute Manager works with John differently than he does with either you or Larry?" asked the entrepreneur.

"He sure does," said Cindy. "John is at another location. But my assistant can probably set up a call with him. He's pretty flexible. In his role, he has to be available to work on a moment's notice with whatever comes up."

"I would really appreciate her setting up a call," said the entrepreneur. "Thanks for your help."

Cindy's assistant reached out to John DaLapa's office and was told John was talking with the One Minute Manager through video conference. John said he would be happy to have the entrepreneur join their call, so Cindy's assistant helped the entrepreneur dial into the video conference.

Once the entrepreneur was on the video call, the One Minute Manager laughed and said to her, "I'd better be on my way, or you'll think I'm prejudicing your sample."

"He doesn't scare me," John said to the entrepreneur with a smile. "I'll tell you the real truth."

The One Minute Manager was laughing as he left the call.

The entrepreneur admired the open, supportive atmosphere she found in the company. Everyone seemed to enjoy and respect one another.

"What can I do for you?" John asked.

"Cindy Liu says that the One Minute Manager leads you differently than the way he manages Larry McKenzie or her. Is that true?"

"Well, I don't know about that," said John. "It's not easy for me to describe his style."

"What do you mean?" asked the entrepreneur.

"My job is relatively complicated," John said. "I'm ultimately responsible for all production. That means I design and lead each part of the operation. I'm also responsible for quality control, as well as for hiring and developing the entire operations team. What I find is that the One Minute Manager uses one style with me on certain parts of my job and another style with me on other parts. For example, on the pure operations end of my job he literally leaves me alone, but it took him a while before he would do that. The One Minute Manager built this company from the ground up. Because he knows the operations side of the business as well as I do, he's come to respect and trust my judgment on operational matters. Now he just says, 'Keep me informed, but that's your area—you run with the ball. You're the technical expert around here.'"

"You mean he doesn't discuss things with you or tell you what to do or tell you how to solve a particular problem?" questioned the entrepreneur.

"No," said John. "Not as far as the technical part of my job goes. But his style is completely different when it comes to the people part of my job. He insists that I consult with him before I implement any new programs or policies that affect people. He wants to know exactly what I intend to do."

"Does he tell you what to do in those areas?" asked the entrepreneur.

"He always tells me his opinion," said John, "if that's what you mean. But he usually asks mine, too."

"If there is a difference in your opinions and you can't come to an agreement, who decides?" wondered the entrepreneur.

"The One Minute Manager decides."

The entrepreneur made a note to herself to come back to that comment.

"Is it disconcerting when he treats you one way sometimes and another way at other times?" asked the entrepreneur.

"Not at all," said John. "I just love the freedom he gives me on the operations part of my job. After all, I started as a technician here and worked my way up the ladder to my present position. Over the twenty years I've been here, I have always kept on top of our technology."

"Wouldn't you like to be treated the same way in the people area?" asked the entrepreneur.

"Not really," said John. "With people I'm sometimes like a bull in a china shop. In fact, some people claim I knock down the door and then ask if I can come in. So I'm not always confident about my interpersonal skills. That's why I welcome the One Minute Manager's suggestions."

"It sounds like the One Minute Manager is pretty flexible," said the entrepreneur. "But isn't that kind of confusing? How do you know what you're going to get?"

"Because we talk about the leadership style I need. Most of the time, we're on the same page. Not always, but most of the time," said John with a laugh.

"So what would you call him if he's not consistent or predictable?" asked the entrepreneur.

"A situational leader," said John. "He changes his style, depending on the person he is working with and on the situation."

A situational leader. The phrase kept spinning around the entrepreneur's head as she hurried to her afternoon meeting with the One Minute Manager.

"Well, how did I do?" asked the One Minute Manager.

"Just fine," said the entrepreneur. "Your philosophy of Different Strokes for Different Folks is alive and well. And what's more, your folks don't seem to mind being treated differently. How can I become a situational leader?"

"You need to learn three skills," said the One Minute Manager.

"I knew you would have it down to some simple formula," the entrepreneur teased.

The One Minute Manager chuckled. "I'm not sure it's so simple, but there are three skills involved. You have to learn how to set clear goals. You have to learn how to diagnose the development levels of the people you work with on each of their goals. I'll tell you more about that in a minute. Finally, you have to learn to use a variety of leadership styles to provide individuals with what they need from you. So, the three skills are: *goal setting*, *diagnosis*, and *matching*."

"Sounds challenging," said the entrepreneur.

"It's not hard once you learn the basics," replied the One Minute Manager. "After a time it becomes second nature."

"Where do I start?"

"At the beginning—with goal setting," said the One Minute Manager. "That makes sense, since the first secret of One Minute Management is One Minute Goal Setting. All good performance starts with clear goals."

"I realize goal setting is important, but I'm sure I could learn a lot more about it from you," said the entrepreneur.

"Maybe, but why don't you go see Randy Rodriguez in our people and talent development group?" said the One Minute Manager. "If you're available, I'll try to set something up for tomorrow morning."

"I'll make the time," said the entrepreneur. "I'm eager to learn."

The One Minute Manager smiled and said, "Randy has designed our company's performance management system, and I think he is the best person to talk with you about goal setting."

"That sounds good," said the entrepreneur. "I love the fact that you have a people department."

"So do our people," said the One Minute Manager, laughing.

WHEN the entrepreneur met with Randy Rodriguez in his office the next morning, she told him, "The One Minute Manager said you were the best person to teach me about goal setting."

"I'd be happy to do that," said Randy. "Let me see if I can put goal setting into context. In addition to doing your own job, you have to manage the performance of your people. We talk about three parts to performance management:

1. Performance Planning

2. Day-to-Day Coaching

3. Performance Evaluation

"Goal setting is a key part of performance planning and sets up day-to-day coaching. Yet which of those three parts of managing performance do most companies start with when they develop a performance management system?" asked Randy.

"Performance evaluation," the entrepreneur said. "Most companies develop a form for performance evaluation."

"Then, once these companies have their evaluation form in place," said Randy, "they usually move to performance planning—they require people to write goals. They fill notebooks with goals that nobody ever looks at."

"How right you are," said the entrepreneur. "But One Minute Goal Setting has helped. All the unnecessary paperwork is eliminated when people set only three to five goals."

"It certainly is," said Randy. "But let me ask you another question. Which of the three parts of managing performance—planning, day-to-day coaching, and evaluation—almost never gets done in most organizations?"

"Day-to-day coaching," said the entrepreneur.

"Right," said Randy, "but it's probably the most important part of the process. Yet most leaders and organizations neglect to do it. The importance of day-to-day coaching comes to mind when I think of my favorite college teacher. He was always getting into trouble with the dean and other faculty members because on the first day of class he would hand out the final examination. The rest of the faculty would say, 'What are you doing?' He'd say, 'I thought we were supposed to teach these students.' They'd say, 'You are, but don't give them the questions for the final exam.' He'd say, 'Not only am I going to give them the questions for the final exam, but what do you think I'm going to teach them all semester?'"

"He would teach them the answers," said the entrepreneur with a laugh.

"Absolutely," said Randy. "So when it came to the final exam, the students got As because they knew the answers."

"It sounds as if your teacher wanted the students to do well on the final because they'd learned what he'd taught," said the entrepreneur.

"That's what day-to-day coaching is all about," said Randy, "being responsive to the people you lead. Once your people are clear on their goals—they have the final exam questions—it's your job to do everything you can to help them accomplish those goals—learn the answers—so that when it comes to performance evaluation—the final examination—they get high ratings—As."

"That's a beautiful example of creating a 'win-win' situation for your people," said the entrepreneur. "But how does that relate to goal setting?"

"Without clear goals—what an A looks like—you can't do effective day-to-day coaching," said Randy.

"COULD you give me an example of setting clear goals?" asked the entrepreneur.

"Suppose you were my comp and benefits administrator. The process would start with us first looking at the organization's goals. Next we'd look at your team's goals, and then we'd discuss three to five goals for you."

"Would we have a meeting to reach agreement on my goals?" the entrepreneur asked.

"Yes," said Randy. "That's the first part of what we call an *alignment conversation*."

"An alignment conversation?" asked the entrepreneur.

"Yes. During that conversation we'd agree not only on your goals but also on the performance standards for each goal," said Randy.

"So we'd agree on what a good job looks like," said the entrepreneur.

"Exactly," said Randy. "We'd also rewrite each goal so it was SMART."

"What do you mean by SMART?" asked the entrepreneur.

"It's an acronym. The S stands for *specific*. Goals should state exactly what the person is responsible for and when it needs to be done," said Randy.

"Is establishing performance standards part of the S?"

"No," said Randy. "How performance is going to be measured is the T, which stands for *trackable*. And that's the order in which SMART goals are written—S, then T. You decide specifically what you want the person to do—the S—and then how you're going to track or measure progress toward goal accomplishment—the T. Then you use the other three SMART criteria—the R, A, and M— to check if the goal is truly SMART."

"Tell me about those criteria," said the entrepreneur.

"The R stands for *relevant*," Randy explained. "A goal is relevant if it addresses an activity that makes a difference for the organization and the individual. It feels like it's important work."

"I can see that," said the entrepreneur.

"Next, the A in SMART stands for *attainable*. The goals have to be reasonable. Whether or not they're reasonable depends on what's happened in the past."

The entrepreneur nodded. "Too many companies set goals that are impossible. I'm struggling with that in my own company," she said. "I know what I would like to achieve, but it's probably not realistic in the first few years. I suppose it's the same for individuals. You want to stretch them, but you don't want to make the goals so difficult that they're unattainable and people lose commitment."

"That's right," said Randy. "Finally, the M in the SMART model stands for ***motivating***. For people to do their best work, the goals that are set need to tap into what your team members enjoy doing. We focus on creating the optimal conditions for motivation here. Are people learning and becoming more competent? Are they connected to their work and each other? Are they given autonomy commensurate with their competence? Those are important questions to ask."

"There's no way I'm going to remember all that," the entrepreneur said with a smile.

"I've got something here that can help you with that." Finding what he wanted on his tablet, Randy showed the entrepreneur:

SMART goals answer these questions:

Specific

- What exactly is the goal or task?
- When does the goal or task need to be accomplished?

Motivating

- Is the goal or task meaningful for the individual?
- Will working on this goal build competence and commitment?
- Will working on this goal add or drain energy?

Attainable

- Is the goal realistic, reasonable, and achievable?
- Is the goal within the individual's control?

Relevant

- Is the goal or task meaningful work for the organization?
- Is the goal or task aligned with organization and work team goals?
- Is the goal or task a high priority in relation to other goals?

Trackable

- What does a good job look like, at each level of development?
- How will progress and results be measured and tracked?

SMART goals motivate. They get leaders and the people they lead on the same page.

"Would you e-mail that to me?" asked the entrepreneur.

"Sure. What's your e-mail address?"

"Entrepreneur@SLX.com," she replied.

"I think I really get the power of setting SMART goals," said the entrepreneur. "But what if there's disagreement about one of the goals and after some dialogue, the disagreement doesn't seem resolvable? Who decides?"

"The Golden Rule," said Randy.

"The Golden Rule?" echoed the entrepreneur.

"Whoever owns the gold makes the rules," said Randy with a laugh. "The leader decides."

"Really?"

"Not really," said Randy, "I'm just joking. Goal setting is actually a collaborative process. Remember, the responsibility for making sure that clear goals are set lies with the leader, but the more competent the individual , the more you want their voice to be part of the goal setting process. By aligning on SMART goals you set up the conditions for effective day-to-day coaching."

"I imagine some leaders set goals and then neglect to provide day-to-day coaching," said the entrepreneur.

"You're a fast learner," said Randy. "Without effective day-to-day coaching—especially for people who can't provide their own direction and support—goal setting becomes a license for managers to use the 'leave alone-zap' leadership style."

"The what?"

"The 'leave alone-zap' leadership style," said Randy with a smile. "The One Minute Manager now calls it 'seagull management.' After goal setting, seagull managers are never around until you make a mistake. Then they fly in, make a lot of noise, dump on everybody, and fly out."

The entrepreneur and Randy had a good laugh, because they both knew how true that was.

"Now that I understand goal setting," said the entrepreneur, "how do I learn more about day-to-day coaching?"

"Coaching begins with the second skill of a situational leader: ***diagnosis***. I talked to the One Minute Manager before you came to my office, and he suggested I put you in touch with Kathy Gupta, who leads our IT Group, to learn about diagnosis."

KATHY Gupta looked up from her desk when the entrepreneur arrived. "You must be the one who wants to work on your diagnostic skills," Kathy said with a smile.

The entrepreneur nodded. "Randy Rodriguez taught me all about goal setting. The One Minute Manager says that the second skill I need to learn to be an effective situational leader is diagnosing."

"That's right," said Kathy. "Once SMART goals are set and you and your team member are aligned on them, the next step is diagnosing an individual's development level on a specific goal or task."

"Is a person's past performance a key factor in diagnosing development level?" asked the entrepreneur.

"Absolutely," said Kathy. "You need to look at two factors to determine a person's development level: competence and commitment. In other words, anytime a person is not performing well without your direction, it is usually a competence problem, a commitment problem, or both."

"How do you tell whether a person has the competence to do a job?" the entrepreneur wondered.

"Competence is a function of demonstrated knowledge and skills, which can be gained through learning and/or experience," said Kathy.

"Isn't competence just another word for ability?" asked the entrepreneur.

"Not really," said Kathy. "People often use the word ability to mean potential. They talk about 'natural' ability to describe why some people seem to be able to learn certain skills so easily. Competence, on the other hand, can be developed with direction and support. It's not something you're born with. It's something that is learned.

"Another aspect of competence," Kathy continued, "involves transferable skills like planning, problem solving, and time management skills."

"You mean skills that you can apply to a variety of tasks?"

"Exactly," said Kathy.

"That makes sense. People can leverage the general skills they have in a new situation. What about a person's commitment? How do you measure that?" asked the entrepreneur.

"Commitment is a combination of confidence and motivation. Confidence is a measure of a person's self-assuredness—a feeling of being able to do a task well without much direction—whereas motivation is a person's interest in and enthusiasm for doing a task well."

"Are there times when a person has the competence and confidence to do a task, but no interest?" asked the entrepreneur.

"Yes," said Kathy. "Sometimes people lose motivation when they realize it is going to be harder than they thought. Or maybe they feel their efforts and progress aren't being acknowledged. At other times, people just get bored—they figure the effort isn't worth it."

"I would imagine people can have various combinations of competence and commitment," said the entrepreneur.

"Good point," said Kathy. "You need to remember two things here. First, as you suspected, there are different combinations of competence and commitment. To be precise, four combinations of competence and commitment make up what we call the four development levels. Second, it's important to recognize that development level is goal- or task-specific. It is not an overall rating of an individual's skills or attitude. People can be at one level of development on one task and at another level of development on the next task."

"Can you tell me more about the four development levels?"

Kathy brought up a graphic on her computer. "Maybe this can help," she said.

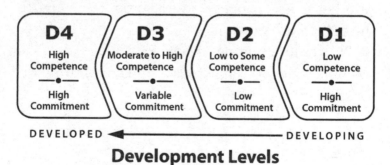

Development Levels

As the entrepreneur looked at the graphic, she noticed that the development level continuum was divided into four segments: D1, D2, D3, and D4. "What's the difference among these four development levels?" she asked.

"When you are D1 on a particular goal or task, you are known as an ***enthusiastic beginner***," said Kathy. "Though you have high commitment, you are inexperienced. You are new to the task or goal. In many ways, you don't know what you don't know. Therefore you are low on competence."

"Does the enthusiasm and high commitment come from an eagerness to learn?"

"Absolutely," said Kathy. "You are excited and curious, and fairly confident that learning won't be difficult. You're counting on your transferable skills to help you learn quickly. You don't think learning will be difficult."

"That describes me perfectly," said the entrepreneur, "in terms of learning how to be a situational leader."

"Don't be surprised if you soon become a D2— or what we call a ***disillusioned learner***," said Kathy with a laugh.

"That doesn't sound good," said the entrepreneur.

"It's not good or bad being a D2," said Kathy. "It's just a stage of development. If you became a D2, you would have low to some competence, because you now have some knowledge and skills. But you might find there's more to learning about being a situational leader than you thought, so you haven't made as much progress as expected."

"I'm guessing that could lower my commitment," said the entrepreneur.

"Yes," said Kathy. "If you became a D2, you could become frustrated and may even be ready to quit."

"I don't think I'd give up that easily," said the entrepreneur.

"Maybe not," Kathy replied. "But you'd want to understand a lot more about the whys behind the whats, hows, and whens. You'd want perspective; you'd want to know if you were making progress. And you'd want encouragement."

"Tell me about the D3 development level."

"We call D3s *capable but cautious* contributors. They have demonstrated some competence and experience in doing the task, but they lack confidence in doing that task by themselves. They can be self-critical and unsure. They can also be bored with a particular goal or task and lose commitment that way."

"What about D4s?" asked the entrepreneur.

"If you become a D4 in your learning to be a situational leader you'll be a *self-reliant achiever*. You will have both high competence and commitment."

"Now that you've made it clear," said the entrepreneur, "I can see that people who are at different levels of development need to be treated differently."

"They do," said Kathy. "I'm glad that makes sense."

"I would imagine that the people who can work independently—without much direction—are at development levels D3 or D4," said the entrepreneur.

"Exactly!" said Kathy. "When they're at those development levels, they have demonstrated the necessary skills and knowledge to perform at a high level. The difference between a D4 and a D3 is commitment. If there's low confidence, a D3 needs good questions. They need someone to listen to them. They need to hear their own voice so they begin to trust their knowledge and skills. They need support and encouragement. If the D3 has low motivation, the leader needs to listen even more and facilitate problem solving. The person probably knows why he or she is no longer motivated. You have to enlist them in figuring out what's wrong and coming up with a solution. They need to know how important their contributions are.

"A D4, however, is confident and self-motivated. People at this development level need to be valued for their contributions, but they also need opportunities for growth and influence. Because they are competent and committed, they don't require much direction or support."

"Probably all they need to know is what the goals are," said the entrepreneur. "I'd like D4s on my team. Why would you even want to hire people at the other development levels?"

"Because good performers are hard to find, and things change so much, it's hard to stay at D4 on a particular goal or task," said Kathy. "As a result, you continually have to develop people to be good performers, and that involves good diagnostic skills. One of our favorite sayings around here is:

*

*Everyone Has
Peak Performance
Potential—
You Just
Need To Know
Where They Are Coming From
And
Meet Them
There*

*

"So what you mean," said the entrepreneur "is that all of us have potential that can be developed."

"Right," said Kathy. "There's nothing negative about being at a D1 or D2 level of development. All of us have been at those levels of development sometime in our lives on some task we have been assigned or some skill we were trying to learn. Since we'd never done the task before, we initially lacked the skills to perform at a high level without direction or support. Our competence had to be developed."

"It seems that the difference between the other two development levels—D1 and D2—is also commitment," said the entrepreneur.

"That's true," said Kathy. "People at these two levels of development (D1 and D2 on a specific goal or task) lack competence and thus the necessary skills and experience to perform at a high level without direction. But the D1 is motivated, while the D2 is not. The D1's high commitment comes from an initial sense of excitement about learning something new and from the acknowledgment they should get for their transferable skills, initiative, and enthusiasm. A D1 can also be extremely confident, although it may be a false sense of confidence. The D1 is betting too much on their transferable skills to help them accomplish the goal. They are not fully cognizant of what it will take to be fully competent and self-sufficient.

"Sometimes as people's skills grow, their confidence and motivation drop," continued Kathy. "They begin to realize how much more they've got to learn to be able to do a really good job. It's like the old saying: 'The More I Know, The More I Realize I Don't Know.' With encouragement and direction—and a chance to be involved in decision making—a D2's confidence begins to go back up, as he or she gets positive feedback on results."

"I would imagine someone at D1 could be more dangerous without supervision than a D2 is," said the entrepreneur.

"Why do you say that?" asked Kathy.

"Because," said the entrepreneur, "if you leave alone someone who is enthusiastic and confident—but who lacks ability and experience—they'll fail with vigor. Such a person will rush in where angels fear to tread."

"Good point," said Kathy. "If you leave a D2 alone, that person will probably not act without further direction and support, because he or she is stuck and lacks the self-confidence or motivation to take the next step. But a confident person without the necessary competence may not be as cautious."

"I'm already getting a feel for what leadership style would be appropriate for each development level—each combination of competence and commitment," said the entrepreneur.

"Before we get into talking about what leadership style would be appropriate for each development level, remember what I said earlier: Development level is goal- or task-specific. That's why we have modified the saying you might have seen in the One Minute Manager's office to read:

*

*Different Strokes
For The Same Folks
On Different Parts
Of Their Job*

*

"I remember you said that people tend to be at different levels of development depending on the specific tasks or goals they are working on," said the entrepreneur, thinking back to her conversation with John DaLapa.

"Precisely," said Kathy. "Once you and your team member have agreed on three to five goals, then together you have to analyze that person's development level on each of the agreed-upon goals. For example, let's say that an engineer is competent and confident—D4—about handling the technical aspects of her job, but has not demonstrated that same degree of development when it comes to managing her budget. She's a disillusioned learner (D2) on that task."

"So I would imagine you'd have to use a different leadership style for her in each of those two areas," said the entrepreneur. "I got to see that in action when I visited with John DaLapa. Still, I'm not entirely clear on how to use the right leadership style for each development level."

"Why don't you go back and see the One Minute Manager? He can teach you about the third skill of an effective situational leader—*matching*."

"I'd love to hear his thoughts on that," said the entrepreneur, glancing at her watch. "I have to make some calls this afternoon, but I'll see if I can get a meeting with him tomorrow morning. Thanks for your help."

"It was my pleasure," said Kathy.

WHEN the entrepreneur got to the One Minute Manager's office for their scheduled meeting the next morning, she shared her excitement about what she'd been learning.

"It's great to see your enthusiasm," said the One Minute Manager. "How can I help you with your next steps on your journey to becoming an effective situational leader?"

"Kathy Gupta tells me you enjoy teaching people about the third skill of a situational leader—matching," said the entrepreneur.

"I do," said the One Minute Manager. "That's why yesterday I sent you right away to talk to some of my people—to find out about the different leadership styles I use with them. You see, matching is using a variety of leadership styles—comfortably—to provide individuals with what they need, when they need it."

"Speaking of that, I thought I had a handle on your leadership styles until I talked to John DaLapa," said the entrepreneur.

"What do you mean?" asked the One Minute Manager.

"I thought you were either a directive or supportive leader," said the entrepreneur, "but that didn't fit with John DaLapa."

"That always surprises people," said the One Minute Manager. "For a long time people thought there were only two leadership styles. In fact, people used to shout at each other from these two extremes, insisting that one style was better than the other. Supportive managers were accused of being too soft and easy. They were too collaborative, while their directive counterparts were often called too controlling. But I have always felt that managers who restricted themselves to either extreme were only half a manager."

"What makes someone a whole manager?" asked the entrepreneur with a smile.

"A whole manager is flexible and able to use the four different leadership styles." The One Minute Manager brought up a document on his computer:

THE FOUR LEADERSHIP STYLES: A SUMMARY

STYLE 1—DIRECTING

High Directive Behavior and Low Supportive Behavior
The leader provides specific direction about goals, shows and tells how, and closely monitors the individual's performance in order to provide frequent feedback on results.

STYLE 2—COACHING

High Directive Behavior and High Supportive Behavior
The leader continues to direct goal or task accomplishment but also explains why, solicits suggestions, and begins to encourage involvement in decision making.

STYLE 3—SUPPORTING

Low Directive Behavior and High Supportive Behavior
The leader and the individual make decisions together. The role of the leader is to facilitate, listen, draw out, encourage, and support.

STYLE 4—DELEGATING

Low Directive Behavior and Low Supportive Behavior
The individual makes most of the decisions about what, how, and when. The role of the leader is to value the individual's contributions and support his or her growth.

As the entrepreneur studied the information, the One Minute Manager explained it.

"These four leadership styles consist of different combinations of two basic leader behaviors that a manager can use when trying to influence someone else: ***directive behavior*** and ***supportive behavior***. Four words can be used to define directive behavior: decide, teach, observe, and provide frequent feedback. Different words are used to describe supportive behavior: listen, involve, facilitate, and encourage."

"Directive behavior seems to be related to control," said the entrepreneur.

"Somewhat," said the One Minute Manager. "You tell the person what, when, where, and how to do something and then you closely monitor the person on the goal or task. But you also want to acknowledge their transferable skills, their initiative, and their willingness to learn."

"That sounds exactly like the way you are managing your young vice president of people and talent, Larry McKenzie," said the entrepreneur. "You're using a Style 1. I bet you love working with him because he wants to learn and you see his potential."

"You're right, for sure," said the One Minute Manager. "So just to recap, we refer to Style 1 as *directing* because when you use that style you are high on directive behavior but low on supportive behavior. You tell the person what the goal is and what a good job looks like, but you also lay out a step-by-step plan about how the task is to be accomplished. You solve the problem. You make most of the decisions; the person you're leading is responsible for following your direction or plan. You provide feedback and try to leverage the person's willingness to learn and transferable skills."

"But that's not the style you've been using with your finance director, Cindy Liu. You've been more supportive, much more collaborative."

"You've got it," said the One Minute Manager. "That's why we call Style 3—which is high on supportive behavior but low on directive behavior—*supporting*. You support your people's efforts, listen to their suggestions, and ask good questions to build their confidence in their competence. If you need to reignite their motivation, make sure they know how much you value their contributions. You challenge them to excel. Rarely do Style 3 managers talk about how they would go about solving a particular problem or accomplishing a particular task. They help their people reach their own solutions by asking questions that expand people's thinking and encourage risk taking."

"I learned from Kathy Gupta that people at different levels of development need to be treated differently. But do you ever get criticized for being inconsistent—treating Larry one way and Cindy another, not to mention John?" asked the entrepreneur.

"I believe in being consistent, but I think I have a different definition of consistency. It sounds as if your definition is 'using the same leadership style all the time.'"

The entrepreneur thought about that for a moment. "But don't people think it's unfair to treat people differently?" she asked.

The One Minute Manager pointed to a plaque on the wall.

*

There Is Nothing
So Unequal
As The Equal Treatment
Of
Unequals

*

"You must be a fan of Emerson," said the entrepreneur. "He said, 'A foolish consistency is the hobgoblin of little minds.'"

The One Minute Manager smiled. "That's always been one of my favorite sayings. As a situational leader, I've come to believe it's foolish to apply the same style in every situation."

"Just to clarify in my mind the four styles you described, could you give me an example of each?" asked the entrepreneur.

"Sure," said the One Minute Manager. "Suppose there was some noise in the outside office that was bothering us. If I said to you, 'Please go out now and get those people to move their conversation down the hall. When you're done with that, check in with me in case there's a problem.' What leadership style would that be?"

"A directing style," said the entrepreneur.

"That's right," said the One Minute Manager. "You'd be using a Style 1."

"I see," said the entrepreneur. "How would you deal with the noise if you wanted to use a Style 2?"

"That's what we call a ***coaching*** style," replied the One Minute Manager. "Coaching combines both direction and support. If I wanted to use a coaching style in handling the noise I would say, 'There's a lot of noise in the outside office that's bothering us. I think you should go outside and ask those people to move their conversation down the hall.' Then I'd ask you if you had any questions or suggestions. If your idea was better than mine, I'd endorse it. If mine was better, I'd explain my thinking."

"So with a coaching style," said the entrepreneur, "you begin to engage in two-way communication by asking for suggestions. Does the manager end up making the final decision?"

"Absolutely," said the One Minute Manager. "But you get input from others. You also provide a lot of support, because some of the ideas they suggest are good and as a manager you always want to reinforce initiative and risk taking. That's where the listening and encouraging comes in. You're trying to teach your people how to evaluate their own work."

"So Style 2 means you consult with the person you're working with. How about a Style 3?"

"That's the supporting style," said the One Minute Manager. "If I wanted to use that style, I'd say something like, 'There's noise in the outside office that's bothering us—what do you think you could do about it?' I might ask an open-ended question or two about your plan, but generally I'd let you decide how to handle the problem."

"What if you were using Style 4—*delegating*?" asked the entrepreneur. "I imagine you would say, 'That noise outside is bothering us. Would you please take care of it?'"

"That would be perfect for a delegating style," said the One Minute Manager. "In Style 4 you are turning over responsibility for day-to-day decision making and problem solving to the person doing the task. So you can see that with the same problem and the same task—to do something about the noise—you can use any of the four leadership styles."

The One Minute Manager pulled up an image on his computer and showed it to the entrepreneur.

Leadership Styles

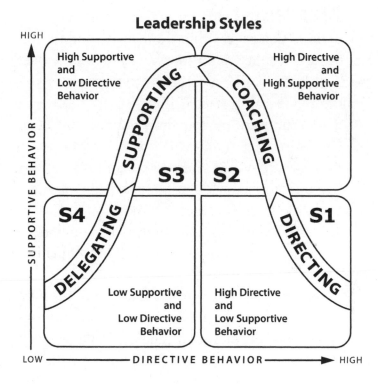

FTER the entrepreneur studied the chart she said, "Before talking to Kathy Gupta and now you, I would have thought there was a 'best' leadership style, like a collaborative or consensus-building leadership style."

"Unfortunately, many people believe that," said the One Minute Manager. "But we feel differently. That's where the word situational comes into play. An S1 supporting style may be a better approach in some situations, but not in others."

"I'm still having trouble imagining when an S1 directing leadership style would be appropriate," said the entrepreneur.

"There are several situations," said the One Minute Manager. "Suppose you were at a meeting and the room burst into flames. Would you ask everyone to break into small groups to discuss what the best way out of the room was, and then have each group report back so the whole group could agree on the best course of action?"

"Absolutely not," said the entrepreneur with a laugh. "I'd say, 'There's the door; everyone follow me.'"

"Exactly. So an S1 directing style is a good match when a decision has to be made quickly and the stakes are high," said the One Minute Manager.

"I'll buy that example," said the entrepreneur. "In what other situations would a directing style be appropriate?"

"Suppose you hire someone who has little experience but you believe has real potential for learning," said the One Minute Manager. "Does it make sense to ask that person what, when, where, and how to do things?"

"Not unless you're interested in wasting time and resources," said the entrepreneur. "I understand what you're getting at now. Directing is also appropriate for inexperienced people who you think have the potential to be self-directed."

"Definitely," said the One Minute Manager. "Directing might also be appropriate for someone who has some skills but doesn't know the company—its priorities, policies, or ways of doing business."

"Don't people often resent direction and close supervision?" wondered the entrepreneur.

"Usually not in the beginning," said the One Minute Manager. "When they are first learning a task, most people—as I'm sure Kathy told you— are enthusiastic beginners. They're ready for any help you can give them. After all, they want to perform well and they want to learn quickly."

"Do you really think people want to perform well?" the entrepreneur asked. "I've observed a lot of people in organizations who appear to be trading time on the job to satisfy needs elsewhere. They seem to be working just for the money. They don't care whether the organization accomplishes its goals or not."

"You're right," said the One Minute Manager. "There are people—too many, I'm sad to say—who don't seem to care and are just putting in time. But if you could go back and observe them when they were first starting a new job, I doubt you would see that lack of commitment. I think people lose their commitment only after they realize that good performance doesn't make a difference."

"What do you mean?" asked the entrepreneur.

"I mean," said the One Minute Manager, "that good performance often goes unrecognized. When people do something well, their managers don't say anything. When they make a mistake, they hear about it right away."

"Randy Rodriguez told me about 'leave alone-zap' or seagull leadership," said the entrepreneur with a smile. "I can sense why that approach wouldn't be very helpful for learners or with anyone, for that matter."

"You're right," said the One Minute Manager. "It's how inexperienced people are managed that causes them to lose their commitment. Once you've lost commitment, providing direction is not enough; you also have to provide support and encouragement."

"Now you're talking about an S2 or coaching style, aren't you?" suggested the entrepreneur.

"Yes," said the One Minute Manager. "A coaching style works best when disillusionment sets in."

"Kathy told me about the disillusioned learner, but I'd like your take on disillusionment," said the entrepreneur.

"Have you noticed," said the One Minute Manager, "that as people begin to work on a task, they often find it harder to master than they thought it was going to be? That's often why they lose interest. Or maybe the drop in commitment comes because they don't think all their efforts are going to pay off. Or maybe they aren't getting the direction they need—in fact, they're continually getting zapped. Or progress is so slow or nonexistent that they lose confidence in their ability to learn to do the task well. When this disillusionment happens—when the initial excitement wears off—the best style is a coaching style, which is high on direction and support."

"You want to continue to direct because they still need to build skills and competence?" the entrepreneur asked.

"Yes," said the One Minute Manager. "But you also want to listen to their concerns, provide perspective, and acknowledge progress. And you want to involve them in decision making as much as you can, because that's how you'll build back their commitment."

"You make it sound as if everyone gets disillusioned at some point when they're learning a new task or taking over a new project."

"Some people more than others," said the One Minute Manager. "It depends on how supportive and available the manager is. But I'm getting ahead of myself."

"Interesting," said the entrepreneur. "So an S1 directing leadership style is better with enthusiastic beginners (D1), whereas an S2 coaching is the right style for disillusioned learners (D2)."

"Right," said the One Minute Manager. "What kind of people do you think dislike directing or coaching?"

"Experienced people," said the entrepreneur. "They would probably like a more supportive or collaborative leadership style."

"You've got it," said the One Minute Manager. "Experienced people like to be listened to and supported. I think you talked to our finance director, Cindy Liu. She responds well to an S3 supporting style on almost every task she's assigned, because even though she's experienced and competent, she's sometimes a capable but cautious performer. When I ask her to take on a project, she has a lot of ideas, but she'll often want to test her ideas out with me first. She wants to be involved in decision making, but she sometimes doesn't have as much faith in her ideas as I do. She needs to build up her confidence or be re-excited about the task, which a supporting style provides. And yet this style is not a universally good style."

"For example?" asked the entrepreneur.

"Here's a classic example with a close friend of mine," said the One Minute Manager. "His marriage was in trouble—he and his wife were putting each other down all the time. Finally, we persuaded them to go for marriage counseling. Then we sat back, figuring we'd done what we could."

"Hadn't you?" asked the entrepreneur.

"No," replied the One Minute Manager. "We didn't ask them what kind of counselor they were going to. They went to a supportive, nondirective counselor."

"Well, what happened?" the entrepreneur wanted to know.

"They paid the counselor two hundred dollars an hour," said the One Minute Manager, "while they screamed and yelled at each other. During those discussions the counselor would do nothing but rub his beard and say, 'Hm, I sense some anger here.' They had three sessions with him and split up."

"What you're suggesting is that they needed a good directive counselor," said the entrepreneur, "one who would tell them exactly what they needed to do to start to turn their marriage around. But I'll bet the counselor they went to was effective with other couples."

"You're right," said the One Minute Manager. "Their counselor was very effective with couples who had problems they could solve themselves, with couples who needed someone who could listen and support them while they problem solved. It sounds as if you're convinced now that there is no one best leadership style."

The entrepreneur smiled. "You're getting to me," she admitted. "But what about S4, delegating? When is that a match?"

"Delegating is appropriate for people who are self-reliant achievers—people who are competent and committed. They don't need much direction, and they're also able to provide their own support," said the One Minute Manager.

"You mean they acknowledge their own contributions and catch themselves doing things right?" asked the entrepreneur.

"In many cases they do," said the One Minute Manager. "When you go to see them, they often take you on 'praising tours'—pointing out all the things they and their people have done right. Top performers don't need much direction or support, as long as they know how well they are doing and what they and their team members are accomplishing. I heard a cute story the other day that emphasizes the importance of delegating."

"What story is that?" asked the entrepreneur.

"I thought you would never ask," said the One Minute Manager with a laugh.

"One day a little girl asked her father, 'Daddy, why does Mommy bring so much work home at night?'

"'Because she doesn't have time to finish it at work,' answered the father.

"In her infinite wisdom the little girl replied, 'Then why don't they put her in a slower group?'"

"THAT'S a great story," the entrepreneur said, laughing. "If the little girl had known about being a situational leader, she could have asked why Mommy didn't delegate more!

"I think I'm convinced now more than ever about the power of the three skills of a situational leader: goal setting, diagnosing, and matching," continued the entrepreneur. "I see how just setting goals with people is not sufficient to guarantee goal attainment. Day-to-day coaching is needed. But there's no best way to help people accomplish their goals. That requires diagnosing the development level of an individual and then matching your leadership style to the amount of direction and support they need to accomplish each goal. If I can learn to apply these three skills, I can become an effective situational leader."

"That's for sure," agreed the One Minute Manager. "And yet most leaders aren't willing to stop for a minute to decide what people need from them. They just keep driving themselves and others. They must have an internal critic who keeps telling them, 'Don't Just Sit There— Do Something!' But I've found this to be true:

*

When
I
Slow Down,
I
Go Faster

*

"So I should think before I act," said the entrepreneur.

"That's what diagnosing and matching are all about," said the One Minute Manager. Let me see if I can put this all together for you."

Get Agreement Statements

D1	"Since you haven't done this before, would it be helpful if I provided you with some direction, resources, and information?"	**S1**
D2	"Since you're still learning, and may be discouraged, would it be helpful if I continued to provide you with some direction? And I'd also like to hear your ideas."	**S2**
D3	"Since you know how to do this, what you need me to do is listen, rather than give advice, right?"	**S3**
D4	"I know you're taking the lead, but I'm here, when and if you need me."	**S4**

The entrepreneur examined the relationship between the four development levels and the four leadership styles. Then she looked up.

"That's a very helpful way to remember the relationships—the *D's* and the *S's* match up. Let me see if I can summarize:

"Directing (Style 1) is for enthusiastic beginners who lack competence but are enthusiastic and committed (D1). They need direction and frequent feedback to get them started and to develop their competence.

"Coaching (Style 2) is for disillusioned learners who have some competence but lack commitment (D2). They need direction and feedback because they're still relatively inexperienced. They also need support and acknowledgment to build their self-confidence and motivation, and involvement in decision making to restore their commitment.

"Supporting (Style 3) is for capable but cautious performers who have competence but lack confidence or motivation (D3). They do not need much direction because of their skills, but support is necessary to bolster their confidence and motivation.

"Delegating (Style 4) is for self-reliant achievers who have both competence and commitment (D4). They are able and willing to work on a project by themselves with little direction or support."

When the One Minute Manager had finished listening to the entrepreneur's summary, he smiled and said, "You learn quickly."

"Thanks for the praising," said the entrepreneur. "But now that I know about the four styles, I have a question: once I determine which leadership style to use with someone, do I always use the same style with that person?"

"Let's head across the street and I'll tell you about that over a cup of coffee."

AFTER they were seated in the coffee shop, the One Minute Manager picked up the conversation again.

"Let me see if I understood your question. You want to know if, once you determine the leadership-style match to use with a person, it is ever appropriate to change that style. Let me give you an example with my son, Tom, which will not only answer your question but also further reinforce that no one is at one development level on all tasks.

"A number of years ago, when our son was in the fifth grade, my wife and I got word that he was a year or so ahead of his class in reading, but a year or so behind in math. When I found out what was happening, I called one of his teachers."

"One of his teachers?" echoed the entrepreneur.

"Yes. There were fifty kids in his class, and four or five teachers worked with them on various subjects. When I went to see the teachers, I asked, 'How do you treat Tom differently in reading versus math?'

"They said, 'What do you mean?'

"I said, 'What do you do during reading?'

"They said, 'Do you see those files on the far wall? Every kid has their own reading file. When it's reading time, the kids go over, get their files out, take them back to their desks, and begin to read where they left off. If they have any questions, they raise a hand, and one of us comes over to help them.'

"What leadership style do you think they were using with Tom in reading?" asked the One Minute Manager.

"Delegating," said the entrepreneur. "He got his own folder and he decided when he needed help."

"What development level do you think he was at in reading?" questioned the One Minute Manager.

"D4, I would imagine," said the entrepreneur.

"Absolutely," said the One Minute Manager. "He loved reading and was very good at it. As a result, a delegating style was right on the money.

"Then I said to the teachers, 'What do you do during math?'

"The teachers said, 'See those files on the other wall? Every kid has their own math file. When it's time for math, the kids go over, get their files out, take them back to their desks, and begin to do their math where they left off. If they have any questions, they raise a hand, and a teacher comes to help them.'

"'How is that working with Tom in math?' I asked.

"'Horribly,' they said. 'We're really worried about him.'

"I said, 'You should be! I'm disappointed in the approach you've been taking with him in math. Didn't anyone ever tell you that you might have to use a different teaching style with the same child in different subjects?'

"What leadership style do you think they were using with Tom in math?"

"Delegating," said the entrepreneur.

"What development level do you think he was at in math?" asked the One Minute Manager.

"A much lower development level, I assume," said the entrepreneur.

"That's right," said the One Minute Manager. "He was a D2. He didn't like math because he wasn't very good at it. As a result, the delegating style wasn't working. In fact, it was more 'abdicating' than delegating."

"Then I asked, 'Which one of you has the reputation of being the most traditional teacher?' An older teacher, Mrs. McBride, smiled. She had been a teacher in the school system for thirty years before her school moved to team teaching. I remember going past Mrs. McBride's classroom one time at twelve-fifteen when she was in a small elementary school that didn't even have a lunchroom. The door was open and thirty fifth graders were sitting quietly at their desks eating their lunches while Mrs. McBride played Beethoven on the record player."

"I'll bet that demonstrated a new definition of control for you," said the entrepreneur.

"It certainly did," said the One Minute Manager, smiling. "Mrs. McBride was a beautiful example of a directive leadership style. Across the hall was the other fifth grade class. The door was shut but there was a little window in the door. I looked through the window, and it looked like a zoo in there. The kids were running all over the place, up on the desks and chairs. Mrs. Jones, the teacher—who is a wonderful person—was hugging and kissing the kids and dancing with them. It looked like a fun place to be. What a contrast!

"Do you think Mrs. Jones would have been a good teacher for Tom in reading?" asked the One Minute Manager.

"Sure," said the entrepreneur.

"Why?"

"Your son didn't need a teacher in reading," said the entrepreneur with a smile.

"That's right," said the One Minute Manager. "When you know what you're doing, you don't need a bossy teacher."

"But if you have to have a teacher in your best subject," the entrepreneur said, laughing, "who wouldn't like a warm, fuzzy one like Mrs. Jones?"

"I said to Mrs. McBride, 'Tom isn't doing very well in math. Could you straighten him out?'

"'Sure I could,' she said.

"'How would you do it?' I inquired.

"'It would have been a lot easier,' said Mrs. McBride, 'if I'd had him from the beginning. I think he's discouraged now because it's harder than he thought it was and he's not doing well. So now when it's time for math I would go over to Tom and say, "It's math time, Tom. Let's go over and get your math folder." (I don't think he even gets his own folder. I think he gets the folders of his friends who are absent just to mess them up.) Then I'd take him back to his desk and say, "Tom, I want you to do problems one through three, and I'll be back in five to ten minutes to talk to you about your answers. If we work on this together, I know you're going to get better at math."'

"I said, 'That's exactly what he needs! Would you please take over his math?'

"And she did," said the One Minute Manager.

"Did Tom do well with Mrs. McBride's coaching style?" wondered the entrepreneur.

"You'd better believe it," said the One Minute Manager. "But do you think he enjoyed all that supervision and control?"

"No," said the entrepreneur.

"That's the one thing I hate to report to the humanists of the world," said the One Minute Manager. "People do not learn skills by love alone."

"What you're saying," said the entrepreneur, "is that if a person doesn't have competence on a particular task, then someone has to direct, control, and supervise that person's behavior, and if that person's commitment is low, you also have to provide support and encouragement."

"Luckily, in Tom's case," said the One Minute Manager, "there were only three months left in the school year. What do you think Mrs. McBride's weakness was?"

"Maybe she was too rigid?" the entrepreneur ventured.

"In a way, yes. She was able to change her style from directing to coaching, but she could never change her style from coaching to supporting and delegating," said the One Minute Manager. "She was great at start-up work, but once kids began to learn their math skills, she wouldn't let them take more responsibility for their own learning."

T HE entrepreneur sipped her coffee and nodded. "You were right," she said. "Your example with your son not only illustrates that development level is goal- or task-specific, but it also makes clear that a leadership style that is appropriate with a person at one moment in time may be inappropriate with the same person later on."

"Definitely," said the One Minute Manager, "particularly when it comes to the directing and coaching styles. Your goal as a manager should be to gradually increase the competence and confidence of your people so that you can begin to use less time-consuming styles—supporting and delegating—and still get high quality results."

"How does that change in leadership style occur?" wondered the entrepreneur.

"First let's look at a model of Situational Leadership® II that shows a combination development level and leadership style."

Situational Leadership® II Model

Leadership Styles

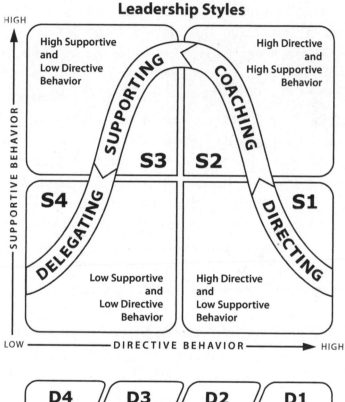

HIGH

SUPPORTIVE BEHAVIOR

S3
High Supportive
and
Low Directive
Behavior

SUPPORTING

COACHING

S2
High Directive
and
High Supportive
Behavior

S4
DELEGATING

S1
DIRECTING

Low Supportive
and
Low Directive
Behavior

High Directive
and
Low Supportive
Behavior

LOW ——————— DIRECTIVE BEHAVIOR ——————▶ HIGH

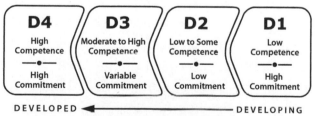

D4	**D3**	**D2**	**D1**
High Competence	Moderate to High Competence	Low to Some Competence	Low Competence
—●—	—●—	—●—	—●—
High Commitment	Variable Commitment	Low Commitment	High Commitment

DEVELOPED ◀———————————————— DEVELOPING

Development Levels

The entrepreneur studied the model closely. "I see the correlation between D1 and S1, D2 and S2, D3 and S3, and D4 and S4. This model certainly makes matching the development level of a person on a particular task with the appropriate leadership style seem easy."

"Absolutely," said the One Minute Manager. "But let me make one other suggestion. In determining what style to use with what development level, just remember that leaders need to do what the people they are leading can't do for themselves at the present moment. Since a D1 has commitment but lacks competence, the leader needs to provide direction (S1-Directing) to help build competence; since a D2 lacks both competence and commitment, the leader has to provide both direction and support (S2-Coaching) to reenergize and re-teach; since a D3 has competence but variable commitment, the leader needs to provide support (S3-Supporting) to build confidence in competence; and since a D4 has both competence and commitment, the leader values their contribution by permitting them to provide their own direction or support (S4-Delegating)."

"That is a helpful suggestion," said the entrepreneur. "But what does the curve running through the four leadership styles mean?"

"We call it a performance curve," said the One Minute Manager. "As development level moves from D1 to D4, the curve shows how a manager's leadership style moves from S1-Directing to S4-Delegating, with first an increase in support (S2), then a decrease in direction (S3), until eventually there's also a decrease in support (S4). At D4 the person is able to direct and support more and more of his or her own work."

"Can you tell me the process a manager uses to change leadership styles?" asked the entrepreneur.

"We teach people five steps to follow when developing a person's competence and commitment."

"I'll bet the first step," said the entrepreneur, "is to tell them what to do."

"Exactly," said the One Minute Manager. "The second step is to show them what to do, to model the behavior. Once people know what to do, they need to know what good performance looks like. They need to know what the performance standards are."

"Those two steps, telling and showing, are the S and T of SMART goals. They are the keys to effective goal setting, aren't they?" asked the entrepreneur.

"Yes," said the One Minute Manager. "Show and tell are also directive behaviors."

"So development usually starts with some directive behaviors," suggested the entrepreneur.

"Absolutely," said the One Minute Manager. "And once goals and directions are clear, the third step in developing people's competence and commitment is to let them try," he added.

"But you don't want to turn over too much responsibility too soon, do you?" wondered the entrepreneur.

"No," said the One Minute Manager. "The risk has to be reasonable. That leads to the fourth step, observing performance. When you use a directing style you need to stay in touch with the person and frequently monitor performance."

"It seems to me that many managers forget this step," said the entrepreneur.

"You're absolutely right," said the One Minute Manager. "Leaders hire people, tell them what to do, and then leave them alone and assume good performance will follow. In other words, they abdicate; they don't delegate."

"From my experience," said the entrepreneur, "unless the people you hire are both competent and committed, they will probably fail, or at least not perform up to the leader's expectations. When that occurs, most leaders, out of frustration, demand to know why things are not getting done or done well. Their demands seem unfair to people who assumed that being left alone meant the leader felt that things were fine."

"So you can see how skipping the observe step can be a disaster," said the One Minute Manager. "That's why we say around here that:

*

*You Can
Expect More
If You
Inspect
More*

*

"I'll bet the emphasis in your inspecting," said the entrepreneur, "is on accentuating the positive."

"Yes, one of my favorite sayings is: If You Want to Develop People, Catch Them Doing Things Right, Not Wrong. That's why the *fifth step* in building people's competence and commitment is first to acknowledge their progress and then second, if no progress is being made, redirection kicks in," said the One Minute Manager.

"Redirection?"

"Yes, you redirect their efforts back to goal setting and then let them try, observe their performance, and finally, acknowledge their progress or redirect."

"That last step applies the second and third secrets of the One Minute Manager—One Minute Praisings and One Minute Redirections," commented the entrepreneur.

"It does, but let me emphasize that praising is the key to helping people move from one development level to another—from D1 to D2, from D2 to D3—until gradually little external support from you is needed."

"I see," said the entrepreneur.

The One Minute Manager nodded. "Let me show you a chart that illustrates exactly what you are saying—how a manager changes his or her behavior as people's performance improves," said the One Minute Manager, pulling out his tablet. He brought up a graphic and showed it to the entrepreneur:

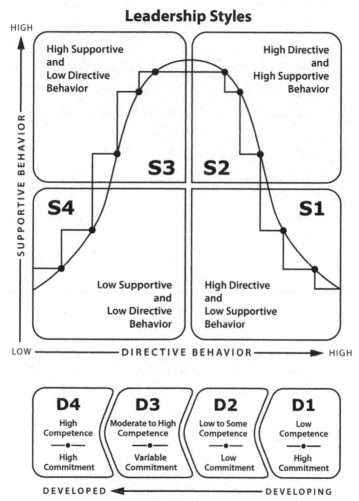

"The steps moving up the curve show how the manager provides less and less direction as the person learns his or her job," said the One Minute Manager. "Initially, more support is provided, but gradually the manager reduces the amount of support she or he provides as well, as shown by the steps going down the curve."

"How can a manager cut back on supportive behavior?" asked the entrepreneur. "Where do the people get their support?"

"From themselves or their colleagues," said the One Minute Manager.

"When managers use a delegating leadership style," wondered the entrepreneur, "does that mean they are providing no direction or support for the person they are leading?"

"The word *no* is too extreme. Even in using a delegating style, some direction and support are provided. But people who are competent and confident to perform at a high level—D4s—are generally not only able to direct their own behavior, but also can catch themselves doing things right, because they've learned how to evaluate their own performance."

"Is your strategy as a leader, then, to change your leadership style over time from directing to coaching to supporting to delegating as performance improves?" asked the entrepreneur.

"Yes, as often as possible. But remember that the fifth step is to acknowledge progress or redirect. So if progress is not being made, I wouldn't acknowledge—instead I'd back up and redirect the person until there's improvement. But my goal is to gradually change my leadership style until my people can perform their jobs well on their own with little direction or support from me. Lao-tzu said it well:

*

*"When The Best Leader's Work
Is Done,
The People Say,
'We Did It Ourselves!'"*

*

"I'D like to be that kind of leader," said the entrepreneur. "But I have a question: what do you do in the beginning when you're first trying to develop someone and the performance is not even approximately right? Do you still praise that person?'"

"No," said the One Minute Manager.

"Do you ignore the poor performance?"

"No. As I suggested, when no progress is being made you redirect by going back to goal setting. You say, 'I made a mistake. I must have given you something to do that you didn't understand. Let's backtrack and start again.'"

"You mean you'd admit you were wrong," asked the entrepreneur, "and redirect the person?"

"Absolutely," said the One Minute Manger. "When you are developing someone, you have to be good at admitting you made a mistake."

"So you're saying that if you care enough," said the entrepreneur, "you will admit that you were wrong and redirect the person. But what if you have to keep directing the person you are training time after time with little improvement in performance?"

"After a while," said the One Minute Manger, "you talk to the person about career planning and outplacement."

"I see," said the entrepreneur with a smile. "So there are some people who cannot be developed on certain tasks."

"Absolutely," said the One Minute Manager.

"I think I can see now why being able to change your leadership style over time—as your people develop their competence and commitment—is an important part of becoming a situational leader," said the entrepreneur. "Right now I'm thinking about a person on my team who used to be competent and committed but whose performance lately has not been up to par. What do I do about that?"

"I would recommend moving from a delegating style back to a supporting style, where you listen and gather data," said the One Minute Manager. "You want to make sure you have the facts and that there are no extenuating circumstances. Sometimes a decline in performance is caused by a drop in confidence—the job is more complicated than anticipated. When that happens, you provide support and encouragement and you engage them in thinking about how to build back their confidence and motivation.

"If you still don't get results," the One Minute Manager continued, "you should move to a coaching style, where you provide some direction, closer supervision, and shorter timelines. Very seldom do you have to move all the way back to a directing style."

"Do you always recommend moving backward through the styles one at a time?" the entrepreneur asked.

"Most of the time," said the One Minute Manager. "Because if, in talking to the person, you gather any new information that explains the poor performance, you can always return to a delegating style without harming your relationship with that person. But if you go straight from a delegating style to a directing style, you are back into seagull management—the old 'leave alone-zap' leadership style. And if there is a good reason for the poor performance, you are standing there with your foot in your mouth."

"I can't thank you enough for what I've learned about being an effective situational leader," said the entrepreneur. "But now that I know about goal setting, diagnosis, and matching, how do I put that to work with my people in the real world?"

"First, you have to teach your people what you're learned from us about situational leadership," said the One Minute Manager. "We feel strongly that:

*

*Situational Leadership
Is Not
Something You Do
To People
It's
Something You Do
With People*

*

"I love that," said the entrepreneur. "So you look at people more as partners. You don't see them as subordinates."

"They're absolutely not subordinary, otherwise we wouldn't have hired them!" said the One Minute Manager. "And I'm not their superior. That's why, if I'm going to be a situational leader, I have to let people know what my intentions are."

"What do you mean?" asked the entrepreneur.

"One of the concerns we've had with people who are learning how to be situational leaders is that they start using the concepts without telling anybody. For example, suppose I analyze your development level on a particular task as D4— I diagnose you as competent and committed. I really don't have to spend much time with you. I might stop coming to see you. After a while, what would you think if you didn't know I was a situational leader?"

"I'd think that something was wrong," said the entrepreneur. "That you didn't care about me anymore. I would feel ignored and unappreciated."

"Precisely," said the One Minute Manager. "The same would be true with someone at the other extreme—someone who was very inexperienced. Suppose I decided that this person needed a lot more direction from me, so I was in there telling him what, when, and how to do things all the time. If I continued to do that, what would he think after a while?"

"He would probably think you were picking on him," said the entrepreneur, "or that you didn't trust him."

"Then if you two ran into each other in the hall," said the One Minute Manager, "and you said you hadn't seen me in a month, the inexperienced person would say, 'No wonder—he's in my office all the time.' Because I hadn't communicated with either of you about my leadership method, in each case what would have been a good diagnosis and appropriate leadership style would be misinterpreted. As an experienced, talented person, you'd think you'd done something wrong and the inexperienced person would probably think I didn't trust him.

"On the other hand," the One Minute Manager continued, "suppose I sat down with you and together we decided that you really didn't need much supervision from me—we agreed that a delegating leadership style would be appropriate. Then when I didn't come to see you, what would you think?"

"I'd think it was fine, because I'd know why you weren't meeting with me. The fact that you weren't supervising me much would really be a compliment about my skills and competencies," said the entrepreneur.

"Right. And if something came up that you needed my advice on, it would be your responsibility to call me."

The One Minute Manager continued, "Suppose the inexperienced person and I sat down together and discussed the leadership style I would use with him. Then how do you think he would feel about my frequent meetings with him?"

"He would feel fine about that," she replied, "because he would know that you were directing and closely supervising him now so that he could develop his skills. Eventually the goal would be for you to be able to leave him alone," said the entrepreneur.

The entrepreneur sat back in her chair and smiled. "I feel a sense of relief hearing these examples about doing situational leadership with your people, not to them," she said. "As you somehow knew when we first met, I used to think that as the business owner, I had to figure everything out by myself. Now I'm eager to learn as much as I can, so I can work closely with my people as a situational leader."

"That brings me to the second way you can apply situational leadership in the real world. Besides teaching them about the concept, you can also improve the quality and quantity of conversations between you and the people you work with," said the One Minute Manager.

"What kind of conversations?"

"ACTUALLY, there are six types of conversations you can have with your people," said the One Minute Manager.

"First are *alignment conversations*, where you get on the same page with the person's goals and development levels, as well as your leadership style on each goal or task. These meetings happen when goals are set in performance planning or when a new project, goal, or task is assigned.

"Next are the four types of *style conversations*—S1, S2, S3, and S4. During these conversations you follow through and provide the leadership style you agreed to in an alignment conversation. These can be scheduled meetings or impromptu conversations. Finally, there are *one-on-one conversations*. These scheduled conversations permit you and your team to reconnect. At these meetings team members bring up whatever is on their minds—whether it's personal or professional. These conversations allow team members to request the leadership response they want from you, be it direction, coaching, support—or maybe they just need to keep you in the loop.

"I assume you're going to tell me about each of the six conversations?"

"Rather than do that, why don't you join me on a call I have tomorrow with some of the global partners who work with me? That way you'll get to find out not only what these conversations are about, but also how they can work with a virtual team. But you'll have to get here early. We start at seven o'clock to accommodate all our different time zones."

"That sounds great," said the entrepreneur. I'll get here bright and early. I'm looking forward to it."

At six-thirty the following morning, the entrepreneur returned to the One Minute Manager's office for the call with his global associates. She was intrigued by the idea of seeing how a situational leader used the six different types of conversations the One Minute Manager had talked about.

The One Minute Manager's assistant escorted the entrepreneur to the media center, where she found the One Minute Manager and an IT specialist getting everything ready for the video chat.

The One Minute Manager greeted the entrepreneur with a smile. "Have a seat. Three of my global partners—Maria Carlos from Buenos Aires, David Cook from London, and Hishan Saleh from Dubai—will be joining us soon via satellite. I think it's going to be helpful for you to hear how we engage in the various types of conversations I would use with each of them as we work together one on one."

A few minutes later the three global partners appeared on the screen and everyone exchanged smiles and hellos.

"Good morning, Maria—and good afternoon David and Hishan," said the One Minute Manager. "I want to introduce you to a young entrepreneur who came to visit me recently because she felt she was doing all the work herself. It was clear to her that she wasn't developing her people so they could expand their responsibilities. She got excited when she found out I'm a situational leader and she's learned all about the three skills—goal setting, diagnosing, and matching. She's now ready to put it all together by seeing how situational leaders improve the quality and quantity of conversations they have with their people."

David Cook smiled brightly. "That's brilliant!" he said.

The One Minute Manager continued, "I told her there are six types of conversations leaders can have with their people. I thought it would be helpful if the three of you could share about how each of you have used these conversations in partnering with me to accomplish the goals we've agreed on for you."

"That sounds like fun," said Hishan.

"In that case, Hishan," said the One Minute Manager, "why don't you explain how we use alignment conversations in our company?"

"I'd love to," said Hishan. "The purpose of an alignment conversation is to focus both the leader and the individual on what is most important. What are the SMART goals that need to be achieved? What is the individual's development level— competence and commitment—to achieve those goals independently, without direction or support? What leadership style will help the individual achieve each goal and develop competence and commitment? Alignment conversations make sure the leader and the person the leader is working with are clear with each other on the answers to these three important questions."

"So it sounds like in an alignment conversation you use all three situational leadership skills—goal setting, diagnosing and matching," commented the entrepreneur.

"I think that will become clear to you," said Hishan.

"Let's start from the very beginning, Hishan," said the entrepreneur. "How do you and the One Minute Manager set SMART goals?"

"We start by looking at what my key responsibilities are going to be," said Hishan. "One of the biggest obstacles to high performance in organizations comes from unclear expectations and accountability."

"I agree," said the entrepreneur.

"When people are asked what they do and their managers are asked what that person does, it is not uncommon for them to give very different answers," said Hishan. "Without agreement up front about your areas of accountability, you could get punished for not doing what you didn't know you were supposed to do in the first place."

The entrepreneur nodded. "I would imagine that once you have agreement on areas of accountability, then you have to determine how you will be evaluated."

"Absolutely," said Hishan. "That's where SMART goals come into play. Together we make sure that every goal is specific and trackable, so that I know exactly what a good job looks like and how we're going to know I'm making progress."

"Then we make sure every goal is relevant," continued Hishan. "I need to know that achieving a goal will pay off for me and the organization. It needs to feel like it's meaningful work. There are so many demands on our time these days. I have to know that if I invest time, it will make a difference."

"I love that you all want each goal to be attainable, so it's realistic and achievable for you," said the entrepreneur.

"That's very important," said Hishan. "I need to be stretched but not overwhelmed. That's why we like to make sure that my goals are motivating—that is, they energize me, build my confidence, and have real meaning."

The entrepreneur turned to the One Minute Manager. "Do you ever invoke the Golden Rule—'he who owns the gold makes the rules'—if there's a disagreement on goals?"

"Not really," said the One Minute Manager. "If we can't agree about a goal or some aspect of it, I encourage us to keep talking until we agree. Let's move on to how the skill of diagnosing plays out in an alignment conversation. "

"Okay," said Hishan. "Once we are clear on goals—on both areas of responsibility and performance standards—then the One Minute Manager and I individually diagnose my development level on each of the goals we agreed on."

"Let me see if I have the concept of 'individually' right," said the entrepreneur. "Does that mean you analyze your own development level?"

"That's right," said Hishan. "And the One Minute Manager will be doing the same thing. Then our task will be to agree on my competence and commitment with respect to each goal. For example, my three main goal areas are people development, operations, and marketing strategy. After we set performance standards in each area, one at a time, we tell each other what we think my development level is in relation to a standard in people development, for example. Then we both express our opinions."

"How does that work?" asked the entrepreneur.

"The rule is, we agree on who goes first," said Hishan. "If I go first, the One Minute Manager's job is to listen to my analysis and then—before he can say anything—he has to tell me what he heard me saying. And I do the same when it's his turn."

"That frees you up to listen to each other, doesn't it?" said the entrepreneur.

"That's right," said Hishan. "Because if one of us, like the One Minute Manager, is more verbal than the other, he will dominate the conversation."

"Moi?" said the One Minute Manager with a smile.

"After both of us have been heard," continued Hishan, "we discuss similarities and differences in our analyses."

"If you can't resolve your differences," said the entrepreneur, "does the Golden Rule ever come into play in this part of an alignment conversation?"

"Definitely not here," said the One Minute Manager. "With development level analysis, the nod goes to my direct report. For example, if Hishan feels he can be left alone—he's a D3 or D4—and I think he needs more direction and support—he's a D2 or D1—we would go along with Hishan's judgment—with one proviso. We'd have to agree on what the results will be for the next month, so we can both observe his performance."

"In that case, I would probably work furiously over the next thirty days to prove that I was right," said Hishan.

"Which is exactly what I want to happen," said the One Minute Manager. "I want Hishan to be right."

"After you have agreed on development level, Hishan," asked the entrepreneur, "do you then agree on the leadership style the One Minute Manager will use with you on that goal?"

"Yes," Hishan replied. "Once the development level is clear, the matching leadership style is pretty clear. At the same time, you have to remember that the leadership style we decide on may be only temporary as the One Minute Manager gradually helps me learn to direct and support myself, if I'm not already there."

"So when you finish an alignment conversation, Hishan should know which leadership style you'll be using with him on each goal, right?" the entrepreneur asked.

"Right," said the One Minute Manager.

"Alignment conversations sound like they're all about performance planning," said the entrepreneur. "Does that mean style conversations are where you get into day-to-day coaching?"

"You've got that right," said the One Minute Manager. "To tell her more about that, I'm going to throw the ball to you, David."

"That's a long toss over the pond, but I'll give it a try," David said with a laugh. "There are four style conversations—S1, S2, S3, or S4."

"How does a style conversation differ from an alignment conversation?" the entrepreneur asked.

"They're focused on the leader delivering on the leadership style that matches the person's development level on a specific goal or task," said David.

"For example," continued David, "if the One Minute Manager and I agree that I need an S4-delegating style on a particular goal, I would be in charge of initiating our S4 style conversation. It might sound like, 'I've got things handled on this, but I want to keep you informed.' In an S4 conversation, I would take the lead. The One Minute Manager's role would be to encourage my creativity, promote my success, and support my growth by providing me with opportunities to teach and mentor others. He'd also acknowledge my competence, commitment, and contribution. Essentially, when I'm a D4, the One Minute Manager trusts my judgment and my right to make decisions about what, how, and when things get done."

The One Minute Manager chimed in, "When I can match David's development level with a Style 4, I'm much less overworked and stressed-out. I can count on a D4 to step up and take on a lot of responsibility."

"I think I'm getting it," said the entrepreneur.

"In an S3 conversation," said the One Minute Manager, "if an issue is raised, my role would be to facilitate problem solving by asking open-ended questions, helping David come up with his own solutions to the problems he's facing. An S3 conversation, if it's a match, could start like this: 'You just want me to listen, right, rather than offer advice?' My role in ongoing Style 3 conversations would be to listen, facilitate self-reliant problem solving by asking good questions, express confidence and encourage, help the D3 reflect on past successes, and acknowledge competence and contributions. The goal over time with S3 conversations is to build his confidence in his competence, so he can become a D4 in this area."

"What if you both had agreed that David needed an S2-Coaching style in a particular area?" asked the entrepreneur.

"In any S2 conversations with the One Minute Manager, he would be in charge," said David. "As a D2, since I'm still learning and a little discouraged—either confused, overwhelmed, or frustrated—I'd want to share my thoughts and get some direction. I'd want advice and some support to hang in there."

"So an S2 conversation is high on both direction and support," said the One Minute Manager. "An agreement to use Style 2 might sound like, 'It seems like you're feeling a little overwhelmed or frustrated. So to help you, I'll continue to provide you with direction. I'd also like to hear your concerns and ideas.' My role in ongoing Style 2 conversations would be to listen, provide perspective, involve the D2 in problem solving, redirect and reteach, provide coaching and feedback, encourage, and support."

David nodded and said, "In an S1 conversation, I'm clear that what I need is lots of direction and a little support. If I get the direction I want, it feels supportive. Because my motivation and confidence are high, I need some acknowledgment but I don't need the high support someone at D2 needs."

"Tell me more about what a Style 1 Conversation sounds like," said the entrepreneur. "I imagine it's awkward."

David replied, "Not really. An agreement to use Style 1 might start like, 'Since you've never done this before, would it be helpful if I provided you with direction and worked with you closely as you learn how to do it?' Once the agreement is reached in a Style 1 alignment conversation, the One Minute Manager acknowledges my enthusiasm, initiative, and transferable skills. He sets goals, priorities, roles, and limits. He develops a plan and provides resources, solutions, information, and ongoing feedback. I relax because it's just what I need."

"You said Style 1 conversations give lots of direction but little support. Tell me more about that. It doesn't sound right," said the entrepreneur.

"It's misleading to think that an S1 conversation has no support," David replied. There is support for my willingness to learn and for the transferable skills I bring to the goal or task. But with little or no experience on the task, I need direction more than I need someone to ask good questions and listen. Style 1 requires a lot of interaction. I'd feel supported if the One Minute Manager actually followed through, stayed connected to me, gave me frequent feedback, and looked for opportunities to reteach or re-explain what I'm learning."

"So the leadership style, once it's determined, establishes the number, frequency, and kind of meetings you have with your people?" said the entrepreneur to the One Minute Manager.

"Yes," said the One Minute Manager. "Suppose I work closely with David on a specific goal for a few weeks and find that he is catching on and starting to perform well in that goal area. What leadership style should I now move to?"

"S2," replied the entrepreneur.

"You're spot on. I'd provide more support, perspective, and the rationale for why we do things the way we do," said the One Minute Manager. "Then if we have a number of S2 conversations over a period of time and David keeps progressing, what will happen next?"

"I would imagine you'd move to S3 conversations and hopefully in time to S4 conversations," the entrepreneur replied.

"Precisely," said the One Minute Manager. "I will keep changing my leadership style as long as David continues to grow and develop, so at the end of the year we have not only a record of his performance but also a sense of his growth as evidenced by changes in the type of leadership conversations we were having."

"What about one-on-one conversations?" asked the entrepreneur.

"Maria, why don't you tell the entrepreneur about those?" said the One Minute Manager.

"I thought you were never going to ask!" said Maria. "I haven't been this quiet in a meeting for years."

Hishan, David, Maria, and the One Minute Manager shared a knowing laugh.

"Getting back to one-on-one conversations," said Maria, "there are some misconceptions about these. When we say 'one-on-one,' we're not talking about a competition, like basketball. In some organizations leaders have one-on-one meetings, but they're dominated by the leader."

Maria continued, "The One Minute Manager and I have virtual one-on-one meetings once every two weeks for fifteen to thirty minutes. He schedules these meetings, but I set the agenda. In these one-on-one conversations, I can talk about whatever is on my mind—goals, personal challenges, updates on projects—or my personal life, problems, successes, questions, or concerns. I can share as much or as little as I want. It's my meeting. What I do is make a list of topics and then think about how I'd like the One Minute Manager to respond. Do I need direction, advice, a sounding board? Or do I just want to provide him with information? It's a meeting that really builds a sense of partnership."

"It sounds like you're really working side by side in these one-on-one conversations," said the entrepreneur. "It doesn't sound hierarchical. I know I have one-on-ones with my team members right now, but they focus on my agenda."

David jumped in. "Yes, but it's important to emphasize that our regularly scheduled one-on-one meetings with the One Minute Manager focus on our agendas—what's on our minds."

Maria nodded and said, "For example, maybe I've heard a rumor and want information. Or maybe I need to discuss with the One Minute Manager how well I'm doing on each of my goals. I might feel I need more or less direction or support. As a D2, I might need advice and some encouragement. Or as a D3, I might need reassurance and encouragement to be more confident in my solutions. Or there might be a need for a change in leadership style. Since the One Minute Manager is so flexible, he can shift styles. He might respond to me with three different styles on three topics in one meeting."

"I think I'm getting the idea of how one-on-one conversations work," said the entrepreneur.

"Good," said Maria with a smile. "We use these meetings to recalibrate. With as much as we have going on, it's easy to forget to follow through on the styles we agreed would help me develop."

"What if something comes up between your regularly scheduled one-on-one meetings?" asked the entrepreneur.

"If I feel I need to reconnect with the One Minute Manager or he feels he needs to reconnect with me outside our scheduled biweekly meetings, we make that happen with impromptu one-on-one conversations," said Maria. "Since we're both tracking the same performance data on my goals, an alarm bell could go off for either of us, which would prompt a meeting. And, of course, if he's agreed to use an S1 or S2 with me, we have a lot of meetings, so he can provide ongoing direction."

"This whole process you're sharing with me certainly guarantees that there will be no surprises come the annual performance review," said the entrepreneur. "At times in my career I couldn't believe how I was being evaluated at the end of the year. These ongoing conversations you have mean that everybody is kept in the loop."

"It's a great way to work together," said Maria. "What I love about situational leadership is that I feel that rather than working for the One Minute Manager, he is working side by side with me to help me succeed."

As the meeting drew to a close, the entrepreneur thanked the One Minute Manager, Hishan, David, and Maria for allowing her to listen in. The three global partners wished the entrepreneur good luck and signed off.

"I can see why you say being a situational leader is the key to being an effective leader," said the entrepreneur. "Are there any other things I should know?"

"I think you know enough," said the One Minute Manager with a smile. "Now you just need the courage to follow through on your good intentions."

"That's easier said than done," said the entrepreneur.

"I suggest we meet about a week after you've had a chance to digest what you've learned here and then periodically after you've started to become a situational leader."

"Next week I'll probably need an S1 conversation. Then hopefully over time you can move from S1 to S2 and finally we can have periodic S3 and S4 conversations," said the entrepreneur.

"Absolutely," said the One Minute Manager. "I wouldn't want to go to a delegating leadership style right away and later learn that you had crashed and burned as a situational leader."

As the entrepreneur walked with the One Minute Manager back to his office, she said, "I'm fascinated by how much sense it makes to be a situational leader. I have to tell you, this is all quite different from what I was taught in the management courses I've taken over the years."

"Different in what way?" wondered the One Minute Manager.

"You make a clear distinction between a leader's attitude and feelings about people and his or her behavior toward them," said the entrepreneur. "We were always taught that when leaders use a directive leadership style, they probably think their people are lazy, unreliable, and irresponsible, and therefore need close supervision. But if leaders use a supportive leadership style, they believe their people are responsible and self-motivated. What I've learned from you is that positive assumptions about people are a given; you believe people have the potential to become high performers. What fluctuates is the leader's behavior, depending on their people's needs for direction and support."

"The key word is potential," said the One Minute Manager.

"That's the beauty of it all," said the entrepreneur. "Now when I use a directive leadership style, I'll know it's not because I think the person isn't talented. On the contrary, I'll think the person has the potential to be a high performer—self-directed and self-motivated—but lacks experience right now. The person needs direction from me to begin developing his or her full potential."

"That's an important lesson," said the One Minute Manager. "What you've learned is that positive assumptions about people can be expressed by using any of the four leadership styles, not just supporting or delegating."

"I think it can all be summarized by this statement," said the entrepreneur.

*

*Everyone
Is A
Potential
High Performer.
Some People
Just Need
A Little Help
Along
The Way*

*

"YOU'VE got it," said the One Minute Manager.

"And now I know it's up to me. Finally, I know how to develop my people so I don't have to do all the work myself," said the entrepreneur.

With that, the entrepreneur shook the One Minute Manager's hand and said, "Thanks for your help."

"The only thanks I need," said the One Minute Manager, "is for you to do it—for you to use what you've learned—and to have it work for you. Remember the old Buddhist saying:

*

To Know
And Not To Use
Is Not Yet To Know!

*

And use it she did. The entrepreneur went back to her company and told all her people what she had learned and they in turn told their people. After she had finished her follow-up conversations with the One Minute Manager, the inevitable happened:

The entrepreneur became a situational leader.

She became a situational leader not because she thought like one or talked like one but because she behaved like one.

First, she had alignment conversations with her people where they set clear goals. She worked with her team members to diagnose their competence and commitment to accomplish each goal without direction and supervision, and together they discussed which leadership style matched the goals.

Then she followed through with style conversations to match the leadership style they had agreed to until enough progress was made to warrant a change in leadership style.

She also conducted regular one-on-one conversations with her team members, as well as spontaneous ones when any of her team members wanted to talk.

Years later, the entrepreneur looked back upon the time she had spent learning to be a situational leader. It had made all the difference in her life at work and at home.

Her original company had now grown into eight separate enterprises. She was the CEO of a holding company, and there was a president for each of her eight companies. While officially those presidents reported to her, they really ran their own shows. Over time, they developed skills in most of their areas of responsibility and more often than not a delegating style worked with them, unless the company moved in a really new direction.

She reflected on how she had helped them on the journey to becoming independent, self-motivated, high-performing managers.

The entrepreneur felt the same kind of success at home with her three children. Now that they were grown up, the entrepreneur enjoyed being their friend more than their mother. Not that she wasn't there when they needed her, but now it was their initiative that triggered her involvement in their lives. It made her feel good that they still wanted to spend time with her.

The entrepreneur was happy and proud that she had learned the three skills of a situational leader—goal setting, diagnosing, and matching. What the entrepreneur had built was an organization in which people's contributions were valued. Her responsive style encouraged others to take risks and responsibility until, in time,

It was hard to distinguish who the entrepreneur was.

Acknowledgments

Since this is a revised and updated edition of *Leadership* and the *One Minute Manager*, we have a new group of people we want to praise who were important to its creation.

First, our product development team: *Jay Campbell, Victoria Cutler, Kim King, Martha Maher, Alan Youngblood, Carman Nemecek,* and *Vicki Halsey.* Without them, we never would have reached this point.

We also want to thank *Martha Lawrence*, our editor and guide throughout this process. Thanks also to *Richard Andrews*, head of our intellectual property department, who paved the way for this new edition. And this book would not have happened without the support of our wonderful editor at William Morrow, *Henry Ferris*. We are so appreciative of Henry for all he does.

We don't want to omit the people who helped us get the first version to press in 1985: *Larry Hughes* at William Morrow and *Margret McBride*, our first literary agent. We also thank our creative friends, *Harvey Mackay* and *Spencer Johnson*. And we haven't forgotten that without the typing skills of *Eleanor Terndrup* and *Vicki Dowden*, this book never would have become a reality. Thanks, Eleanor and Vicki.

For their unconditional love and support—which made a tremendous difference in our lives—we thank our late mothers: *Dorothy Blanchard, Florence Kuiper,* and Irma *Zigarmi*. Finally, we thank our children—*Scott, Debbie, Lisa,* and *Alexa*—for enriching our lives with love.

About the Authors

Few people have made a more positive and lasting impact on the day-to-day management of people and companies than **Ken Blanchard**. He is the coauthor of several best-selling books, including the blockbuster international best seller The *One Minute Manager* and the giant business best sellers *Raving Fans* and *Gung Ho!* His books have combined sales of more than eighteen million copies in more than twenty-seven languages. Ken is the chief spiritual officer of The Ken Blanchard Companies™, a worldwide human resource development company. He is also cofounder of Lead Like Jesus, a nonprofit organization dedicated to inspiring and equipping people to be servant leaders in the marketplace.

Ken received his bachelor's degree in government and philosophy from Cornell University, his master's in sociology and counseling from Colgate University, and a doctorate in educational leadership from Cornell University.

Ken and his wife, Margie, live in San Diego and work with their son Scott, his wife Madeleine, and their daughter Debbie.

Patricia Zigarmi is vice president for business development at The Ken Blanchard Companies. With her leadership, ongoing initiatives for Situational Leadership® II training and coaching have been negotiated with many global companies. She is the product champion and senior author on The Ken Blanchard Companies' SLII® Experience. She is also the coauthor of Blanchard's Leading People Through Change and Leadership Point of View products. Respected for her ability to listen and build trust, she has been a coach to the executives and managers in many companies.

She received her bachelor's degree in sociology from Northwestern University and her doctorate in leadership and organizational behavior from the University of Massachusetts at Amherst.

Drea Zigarmi, formerly president of Zigarmi Associates, Inc., is the director of research and development for The Ken Blanchard Companies. His work has been critical to the organization's success. Almost every product that has been developed at The Ken Blanchard Companies over the last twenty years has Drea Zigarmi's mark on it. He coauthored with Ken Blanchard the well-known "Leader Behavior Analysis" instrument and the "Leadership Action Profile" form used in Situational Leadership® II seminars.

He has coauthored three books: *The Leader Within: Learning Enough about Yourself to Lead Others, The Team Leaders' Idea-a-Day Guide,* and *Leadership and the One Minute Manager.*

He received his bachelor's degree in science from Norwich University and a master's in philosophy and doctorate in administration and organizational behavior from the University of Massachusetts at Amherst.

Services Available

Leadership and the One Minute Manager is part of a trilogy that includes *The One Minute Manager Builds High Performing Teams* and *Self Leadership and the One Minute Manager.* These three books describe the three leadership programs that have played a major role in building The Ken Blanchard Companies.

The Ken Blanchard Companies® is committed to helping leaders and organizations perform at a higher level. The concepts and beliefs presented in this book are just a few of the ways that Ken, his company, and Blanchard International—a global network of world-class consultants, trainers, and coaches—have helped organizations improve workplace productivity, employee satisfaction, and customer loyalty around the world.

If you would like additional information about how to apply these concepts and approaches in your organization, or if you would like information on other services, programs, and products offered by Blanchard International, please contact us at:

The Ken Blanchard Companies
World Headquarters
125 State Place
Escondido, California 92029
United States

Phone: +1–760–489–5005
E-mail: International@kenblanchard.com
Web site: www.kenblanchard.com

United Kingdom
The Ken Blanchard Companies UK
Phone: +44 (0) 1483 456300
E-mail: uk@kenblanchard.com
Web site: www.kenblanchard.com/contactUK

Canada
The Ken Blanchard Companies Canada
Phone: +1 905 829–3510
E-mail: Canada@kenblanchard.com
Website: www.kenblanchard.com/canada

Singapore
The Ken Blanchard Companies Singapore
Phone: +65–6775 1030
E-mail: Singapore@kenblanchard.com
Web site: www.kenblanchard.com/singapore

Australia
Blanchard International Australia
Telephone:+61 2 9858 2822
E-mail: Australia@kenblanchard.com
Web site: www.blanchardinternational.com.au

India
Blanchard International India
Telephone: +91–124–4511970
E-mail: India@kenblanchard.com
Web site: www.blanchardinternational.co.in

Ireland
Blanchard International Ireland
Phone: +353 879614320
E-mail: Ireland@kenblanchard.com
Web site: www.blanchardinternational.ie

New Zealand
Blanchard International New Zealand
Phone: +64 (0) 27 510 5009 / 0800 25 26 24
E-mail: Newzealand@kenblanchard.com
Web site: www.blanchard.co.nz